To Blake
Christmas 1999

THE TRAIL'S PHILOSOPHY

by

Jeremiah Johnson

Illustrations by Larry Bute

NORTEX PRESS ★ AUSTIN, TEXAS

To of all those who have worked cattle
horseback upon the western ranges and to those
who can only do so in their dreams.

All in all, my years on the trail were the happiest I ever lived. There were many hardships and dangers, of course, that called on all a man had of endurance and bravery; but when all went well there was no other life so pleasant. Most of the time we were solitary adventurers in a great land as fresh and new as a spring morning, and we were free and full of the zest of darers.

–Charles Goodnight

FIRST EDITION

Manufactured in the United States of America
By Nortex Press
A Division of Sunbelt Media
Austin, Texas

Praise for Jeremiah Johnson

Is there, I wonder, a finer cowboy poet than young Jeremiah Johnson of . . . Texas? Perhaps, but one thing about his work is apparent. It enlarges the genre. For example, his "For Tombstone" is filled with surprising, often heartrending images of the passing of the West, and what it has meant to us. Still, he reminds us that "Camelot failed. Tombstone stands. Do not forget." Furthermore, Johnson's dramatic delivery enhances the luster of his lines.

Charlie Langdon
Durango (Colorado) Herald

The poetry written by Jeremiah Johnson provides a much needed sophistication to cowboy writing. The intensity and great depth of all his writing is a rejuvenation of the dignified spirit that pervaded most of the early cowboy writers' work—that noble spirit was and is the essence of the cowboy hero. It's refreshing that into the jaded ranks of "cowboy poets" rides young Jeremiah Johnson with his gourmet cowboy poetry. Quality writing by a young man you can respect.

Larry Bute
Cowboy Illustrator

I have had the pleasure of sitting around a campfire with Jeremiah in the high country of Montana. I have seen him perform there and on stage. In "Cowboy Poetry" it is rare to see a performer that reaches his level of thought and intensity. Along the trails of old, Shakespeare was often recited, and readily accepted because of the meter and sounds of the words. I see Jeremiah as the Shakespeare of Cowboy Poetry. Do not expect to read this material once and pass judgment. You'll remember a passage tomorrow that will require you to read it again.

Charlie Camden
Charlie Russell Western Heritage Ass'n.

His prose and rhyming verse transcends the norm of traditional poets in the "Cowboy" genre. He has a keen insight into our cultural heritage and takes his readers or audience onto a plane above and into the world of the true laureate. There is certainly a place for the lighthearted stories of the ranch, prairie, and horse, and then there is art . . . Jeremiah skillfully weaves them all together.

Mark Brooks
Western Entertainer

This impressive young man, Jeremiah Johnson, came to the Arizona Cowboy Poets Gathering in 1998, where he pleased audiences and amazed the other poets with his mellifluous verse. One of the most careful craftsmen among the new generation of cowboy poets, Jeremiah is a wordsmith with few peers who has inherited his craft from the classic poets of cowboy tradition: Badger Clark, Henry Herbert Knibbs, Bruce Kiskaddon.

Warren Miller
Arizona Cowboy Poets Gathering

Jeremiah Johnson brings historical knowledge, personal experience, formidable intellect, and unabashed passion to cowboy poetry, of all things. In his creative hands it is not folk art, it is art.

Sandy Lovejoy,
Editor, KNIX Magazine
Buck Owens Productions

Over the past several years, at gatherings from Arizona to Arkansas, I have found myself on programs with Jeremiah Johnson. The authenticity with which this young man writes is virtually innate, but it was the depth of sensitivity in one so young which first impressed me. I have been privileged to observe the maturity of his writing and presentation. A remarkable talent!

Dee Strickland Johnson
1997 AWA Recipient of
Cowboy Poet–Female Award

This book contains some of the best cowboy poetry by one of our best young poets. His poetry reminds me of some of the greatest works of classical poetry by the bards of an earlier time.

Alvin G. Davis
President, American Cowboy Culture Association
Chairman, National Cowboy Symposium

Young Texan Jeremiah Johnson lives up to the traditions set by D. J. O'Malley, Henry Herbert Knibbs, Charles Badger Clark, S. Omar Barker, Bruce Kiskaddon, Gail Gardner and Larry Chittendon. His verse is in the classic vein. Read and enjoy.

Mike Dawson
Cowboy Poet

Jeremiah Johnson is a young poet with a unique and refreshing style. He presents a picture of how Will Shakespeare might perform poetry if he were a 20th Century Texan. Brilliant!

Staff Sergeant W. J. "Robbie" Robertson
Royal Canadian Mounted Police, Ret'd
"The Mountie Cowboy Poet"

Jeremiah blends cowboy life and Texas history with such passion, the listener is transported back in time. His recitation of his poetry is worthy of the bright lights and rounds of applause.

Stacy Lloyd
EMG Networks

Table of Contents

Foreword

Fifteen years ago Hal Cannon introduced the world to a new category of folk art in an event he called the Cowboy Poetry Gathering at Elko, Nevada. Over the years about every cowboy poet who could put up the money for the trip has made his or her way to Elko in January to listen and learn from the masters. In the years following the first Elko event, gatherings seem to spread across the West, and Red Steagall, the cowboy poet of Texas, started his in the Fort Worth Stockyards. That event successfully completed its eighth year this fall.

Visiting these gatherings over the years, you notice a common thread among most cowboy poets in their experience with ranching and their ability to relate stories that have been passed down through generations. Jeremiah Johnson shares that common thread but takes his poetry to a new level. His use of the language, flair for the dramatic, and untiring search for authenticity has allowed him to create a body of work that exudes a quality far beyond his years.

Jeremiah has a fresh approach to cowboy poetry that can only come from looking at our heritage through the eyes of what many call the "X" generation. He is a treasure that defies his youth and should be nurtured to encourage his work to continue to contribute to the preservation and perpetuation of our cowboy heritage. You will enjoy this collection of poems and narratives that Jeremiah has assembled. As you read them, you should make plans to visit a cowboy gathering near you to hear his delivery of the poetry in person.

Bob Howard
Executive Director
Cowboy Heritage Association of America

Acknowledgments

There never was a herd of cattle driven by one man alone. Instead, it always was an endeavor completed through the efforts of many. I could never have taken these works as far as they have gone without these few people who appear here as no more than names but in reality are so much more. I thank my parents, Sam and Elaine Johnson, whose continual love and support has been my pilot star since my beginning; Chris Lentz, the central Texas cattleman who first gave me a chance at this wonderful way of life; Sandra Palmquist, a teacher who awakened something dormant in my heart so long ago; the late Tex, a horse whose calm demeanor and faithful companionship was the inspiration for many of my works, and all the people that have been before me and seen what I will never see. Yet most of all I give thanks to God, the trail boss who has guided me on this long trail and leads me still, for I feel we have not yet reached our destination.

Introduction

*"May we give hope to the new West
and dignity to the old West"*
–Larry Bute

Inspiration is like a tornado, relentless in its passionate fury, and yet brief in its span of life; it comes when one would least expect it, and often when we would rather choose to shun its presence. But nevertheless, it still arrives, and at this fervor of feeling and thought, the poet must take this storm at its height or what was felt is to be lost forever, never to be felt again.

Such is all poetry, but controversy abounds in the subject concerning the method in which the cowboy poet accomplishes the harnessing of the storm.

When I first took up my pen to write cowboy poetry, I was then unaware that there was even such a genre. The day was clear and magnificent, the twilight sun casting the lush central Texas grass in golden array, and there on a hilltop I sat atop my horse. Even then, I felt the evanescence of ranching in western Bastrop County. Like a slow flood, the electric lights seemed to creep towards my spread, each artificial light seeming to banish another of God's stars from the sky. In that moment, the passion hit me and I began to write. The words flowed like the water in the creeks after a spring rain, as surely towards some climax as a herd heading north to Dodge, and as welcome as the spring sun which makes the grass blush into green with its kiss. What was produced was a captivating poem I dubbed "The Forgotten," a brilliant arrangement of rhyme and emotion. It was after my submission of this poem for a high school poetry project that I learned of the cowboy poetry movement, and beginning at Lubbock, I began to bring my work to North America. Of course, many more works followed, but however great I had thought "The Forgotten" to be, it was not a traditional piece, and therefore no gathering I have attended has heard it. I had written it, as my other works, in the manner that my heart bade me.

Tradition is a force that is of utmost importance to our ranching culture, and thus it remains strong in our poetry as well. It is through tradition that ranching has persevered through the market falls, the iconoclastic ideals of the animal rights activists, and the threat of the removal of ranchers from public land. But, lest we forget, what is now tradition was once a revolutionary idea.

Therefore we must not judge the cowboy poet if he should not choose to write in the ballad stanza so familiar to the genre, or if he should write in blank verse as Shakespeare, or even free verse, although even I must question the suitability of free verse in cowboy poetry.

I think now of the mockingbird I hear outside my window, who sings ascetically for the joy of song, unbound by restrictions, and yet teaching us that should we be despondent during his song, life will proceed. He is in his own way a poet, one more passionate in his song and profound in his message than any human can hope to be. From him we are reminded that we, as ranchers, are also of nature, and it is from nature we should take our example. It is ludicrous to think that someone would ban one bird from singing his song to us because he sings it differently, therefore why should this philosophy adhere to cowboy poetry?

When we have at long last faded away like the trails

before us, there will remain nothing left of us save these writings which we recite on the myriad of stages throughout the world. One can be certain that there will be the numberless film clips, recordings, yet nothing will remain so much as the words themselves. The poets words are the wind to the trees, which bids them whisper when they would be silent, and as compelling as the wind behind the waves moving them to shore. It is also through these words that a person ages hence can obtain a book of cowboy poetry, and speak our words through his own tongue and feel in his unknown age our sorrows, our joys, and our passions.

I feel the works that are gathered in this selection are true glimpses into the inner workings of my soul and represent my best attempt to take that storm of inspiration at it's height. Some can be seen as biographical sketches, while others, such as "The Shadow Man" have been born within the strange world of my dreams. They range from the optimism of "The Trail's Philosophy" to the utter despair of "Hesperus." Then there are those works like "The Chapel" which was wrought both of fancy and reality; conceived in the hill country around Kerrville, yet written in a downtown hotel in San Antonio.

These poems are everything that I am. Read them aloud amidst nature or to your family and perhaps you will feel what I have hoped and dreamed for. Read them inside an apartment above the sweltering city streets and perhaps you will be taken to a world far different. In them, see what I have known and loved: The roar of the Gulf rushing to the shores of Texas, the deafening silence of the Montana highlands, the neighing of horses on a frosty autumn morn; the solemn whisper of the oak upon the prairies that roll like waves upon the sea.

Our Goal

I have always felt an affinity with the passengers of the RMS Titanic. Within the saga of that great ship we observe a parallel of the great western ranching industry; the splendor of a vessel so magnificent that even today it is an endless ecstasy for our imagination.

Never in all the world's history had such a gem been created, although conceived from a pre-existing concept; never before had one vessel gave birth to so many legends, and we set off from the port with a multitude of passengers from every class to surge into the uncertainty of the horizon. Then at a time when most were wrapped in sleep we were struck, perhaps inevitable or due to our own error.

Perhaps we can never know what was our iceberg, for it has long passed and faded into the darkness. We can only stand on the deck and speculate on whether it was the fence, the car, the ideals of an age no longer our own, but then, as the flares explode into the night pleading for help, perhaps it no longer matters.

Therefore we drift aimlessly into the night, our glorious vessel slowly descending into the abyss, stranded without a port to return to, and with no one to hear our cries but silent heaven in the darkness. There have been some who have made it into the boats and regard the dying colossus with sighs of relief mixed among their tears, and there are some who still cling to her, perhaps gallant, perhaps foolish, perhaps against their will but all with no choice left but to face the dreadful imminence of the cold.

Then in the darkness a strain of music softly resounds; the melodies born of a time half forgotten amid the dishevellment when all seemed right within the world. The music is comforting to those who are burdened with their tears, and for a moment, there is order within the realm of chaos. The lights flicker into nothingness, and still the music plays.

Perhaps, as cowboy poets, we are that band whose efforts have been remembered long after the vessel herself has given into both time and decay although within the soul of the world she remains immortal. Ours is the duty of comfort, or remembrance and of hope.

Our vessel is sinking, and there is no way to tell how much longer she will stay adrift.

But the band played on.

The band played on until the very end.

September 8,1998
Goliad, Texas

Come Near

Come near, and listen now with focused ear
And briefly, let your lives with mine exchange;
From modern year and suburbs uncohere,
For past these scenes awaits the open range.
Forget then, that you hear constrained in seat;
Envision that by horse you tread new lands,
And disremember tumult and deceit,
For as you ride, land over land expands.

Thereby our weak divergences recede;
Here glimpse a realm so near but yet aloof,
Suffused with grasses, miles that thought exceed,
And marvel that, known but to God and hoof,
Here midst these hills are sagas yet untold,
And in my verses, let these tales unfold.

A Cowboy's Argument

I hear them say these are the darkest days
For all who herd the cattle with the horse.
The rancher's falling to the veggie craze
And fewer people make beef their main course.
We read their words, we hear them on the news,
Proclaiming that we must not eat the cow.
They sting with words, insisting you refuse
To eat our beef, but eat their tofu chow.
We must not eat the animals, they say,
They are our friends, the wolf and wolverine,
But I observed, and not to my dismay,
I've never seen a wolf that ate a bean.

Now, slowly think of what belongs to him,
This canine predator that lives for meat,
And you will stumble on a fact most grim:
He has some vicious teeth that don't grind wheat.
They're made for chewing, biting on the kill,
And through their food they make a perfect slice.
Why, these dogs can't experience the thrill
Of eating salad with a bowl of rice!
But that dog ain't unhappy with his meat;
Why, he's just had the biggest steak in years!
Don't speak of creature rights if you should meet
This wolf: He won't be shedding any tears.

Now stick your finger in your mouth, that's right!
And slowly feel around inside of there.
Pick out the food that's stuck there from last night
And feel each point and side with utmost care.
But as you feel around, above and underneath,
You'll find something that gives the vegans grief!
And what? What's that? You found some canine teeth?!
All right! It's time for you to eat some beef!
The answer's in the teeth that we need beef
And not just things grown in the ground beneath.
So keep the cowboy herding; eat no leaf,
And eat a steak with your sharp canine teeth!

A Cowboy's Spring Lament

There is this morn rebirth in morning mist,
The fields again the flowers bring,
The trees, they blush again when kissed
When by the passion of the spring,
And yet, for all of this, I grieve, I weep;
These scenes for me hold no serenity,
For you have fled, as when one wakes from sleep;
Oh why, my love, why have you not returned to me?

For all of these do in some seasons part
When hearts grow dry, and pale, and cold,
But they return, should cold depart,
And in that warmth once more unfold.
And should we not to these commandments cling,
We will but wilt the more in winter's sea,
No more to feel what once in us did spring;
Oh why, my love, why have you not returned to me?

Among The Trees

There have been many times that I have slept
Beneath the branches of some massive oak
That stood alone, and only grasses crept
Up to the margin of it's shadowed cloak.
The very isolation of the tree
Would beckon me more near, for to the eye
Enticing are such things, though levity
Of wind was all that brought it where it lie.
Long after I had left, I would recall
The pleasant dreams that wrapped around me then,
The choir of a dozen birds, the fall
Of gentle leaves, and dwell on what had been,
Though never to the others scattered there
Would I take time to lift my eyes and see
The forest whose domain seemed everywhere;
So vast it seemed a separate being to me.

But then there was that time that I had rode
Along the trail that winds into its veil;
The trees like waters in a river flowed
And wind would make the branches seem to wail.
I rode, and nothing yet my path had maimed,
But soon a fallen oak had barred my way.
Gnarled were its boughs, though still a beauty flamed
Within its leaves, and in the falling day
It seemed more like a spirit laid to rest.
Though like none I had ever seen it was,
And far more lovely than those trees unpressed
By others, wind will do just what it does,
And leave us but to mourn with grief to bear
That it took death to notice it was there.

And Now I Leave

And now I leave, though I bear no regret;
Already fades this vision from my memory,
For I may once recall, but find it better to forget
That I was ever in such company.

Therefore I fade as well, and go my weary way
Like one who struggles horseless up a rugged hill
That breathes a breath, though necessary to his stay
That heaves and then exhales in but a second's fill,
To take him one more step than he was at before,
And is remembered then no more.

Death On The Trail

For some it was the first time, other eyes had known too well
The still, the solemn countenance of one dead on the trail.
And now no echo of what had befell remains; no cry,
No gasp for fleeting life, but mournful silence does bely
The clamour, the abandon that was party to this death.
But still, among the notes of elegiac melody
One sound remains, and lingers still when death is memory,
And so it always will when life, when love has fled;
The ignorant and reckless rushing of the River Red.

And so the river surges onward with the solemn trail;
Conceived afar, within whose hearts two equal passions dwell,
And trembling with their force, they grow,
        they rage within their wakes
Until at last convergence comes, and like two angry snakes
They meet, consumed by one another, till at last they pass.
The river rushes still, and thus, though hurt, will life proceed;
The voices softly fade;
        the hooves once more their clatter breed;
The trail moves on, though it be health or wealth
        to which they sped,
And none would know who next would meet the muddy River Red.

Endangered Species

Now up in Bastrop County,
They've got this problem called the Houston Toad.
It's become quite an endangered species
Because it never looks when it crosses the road.
The animal rightists were in an uproar,
Determined this species extinction will beat,
So they went to far drastic measures
And built toad tunnels under the street.

So much money and plenty of time
Was spent to keep our amphibian in the pines.
Why, the little fellow became quite a hero
With it's articles and toad-crossin' signs,
And before the scientists came and told us all,
Few cared for it and even less knew what it was,
But that l'il toad is still among our pines today
Living in the ponds among the moss and fuzz.

But now, it strikes myself as funny
That people use all the time they can find
To save some unknown jumpin' toad
And keep his habitat safe for all his kind.
If folks would look up just to see their kind,
And see the rancher in his spoiled habitat,
Then maybe they would get a better perspective
On where the endangered species are really at.

For Tombstone

There was a time before the blood, before the tears,
This morbid name was not familiar to our ears.
The silver fortunes waited in the hillside crust,
  There was still land still yet to tame
  And Fremont was an unknown name;
An ordinary street of ordinary dust.
But then, on these same streets, on this same sand,
Beneath this very sky, these mountains same,
On these same acres where these buildings stand,
Things changed, and vengeance then to Tombstone came.

All driven by their hate, four men walked on this street,
All armed, all heading for some destiny to meet,
And in an alley, eight men started with a nod
  A fight, so known of by our breath,
  The dragons spit their fire of death,
And thirty seconds found three men reclaimed by God.
The night brought tears and fears, a hate of laws,
A hate of Earps and feuds. The day was gone.
The bodies lowered in Earth's hungry jaws
And still the gunfire echoed on and on

And on. And now, on this same dusty street we wait
With belts no longer burdened by a pistol's weight,
To hear some phantom bullet from a phantom's gun,
  To hear the thunder of the storm,
  To see the spirits rage take form;
How bad we want to rush and see the fight begun!

We wonder what makes this so different from
The rest, for even as we speak, the gun
Has claimed another's life. For them will come
No legend, for the gun's great age is done.

Yet who has never trod this street on which they walked
In their imagination? Who has never stalked
These streets to kill, to end, to set the bullet free
        Into the body of the foe,
        While letting all their anger go,
While devils in the dusty street swirl 'round in glee?
This is our Camelot, worth more in dreams
Than life, it haunts our tales, it haunts our songs,
It lies behind a thousand drama themes,
This town, this Tombstone, in our hearts belongs.

But Camelot fell; cattle graze where blood did rinse,
And now it's mighty walls are but a farmer's fence.
While Tombstone stands, the Western sun begins to set.
        All earthly light must fall to shade
        And all the loudest echoes fade;
The desert screams: Do not forget, do not forget.
When we no longer hear the shots, when we
No longer rush to see the cause of wrath,
When we forget, they die, and cease to be
And then will Tombstone have its epitaph.

Hesperus

The crags cut heaven like a ragged tooth,
The cataract in sorrow seems to weep,
And ebbs the product of her grief to where
Proud Hesperus reclines in ageless sleep.
Oh often, while awash in bleak despair
Did these seduce my eyes in youth.
But now, a weary shadow, scorned and sore,
I, like old men who mourn when lovers kiss,
These view with grief, and sadly reminisce;
Their fairness can delight my eyes no more.

For once in love by these same heights I stood,
A stalwart youth, who age and time defied,
And our loves measure bade my love define.
"Our love is like a mountain," she replied,
"Firm, vast, of incorruptible design
And forged by means scarce understood."
Thereat I beamed, enthralled by this belief
Envisioned clearly through its eloquence,
And so we loved, a fervent confluence
Upon a current mild but brief.

Oh brief, for then to these my eyes were blind,
The fragile peaks by winds discourse laid waste,
The canyon's depth cut by neglected tears,
And thus by these, their bulk to dust debased,
Those which we deem a shape of endless years
Are too a form by time confined.
So lapsed our love, a wealth undone by breath,
And so shall Hesperus bow to abyss,
Felled by a cruel philosophy as this,
Yet certain: love is not so sweet as death.

In An Empty Acre Lot

Beneath the shadows of the clouds that spread
  across this plain,
The NY Ranch now beckons all to recollect her reign.
In your mind recall the herds that thundered in the past,
    The dying echoes of a song;
    The cattle gathered in their throng;
While focused on this peaceful scene, recall the West
  that couldn't last.
Ten hundred cattle graze no more upon this prairie floor,
And all the cowhands now have left;
  there's nothing to explore.
Its glory days are now forgot
    And only this small place remains;
    Just try to think of open plains
In an empty acre lot.

No more! It's gone! There are no open ranges on this place!
The fences came down, then rose a town;
  she stands in fallen grace!
In this lot the last mesquite spreads out its piercing thorns,
    But it shall never prick a hide,
    For nothing grazes by its side;
The cattle bawl here never more;
  hear instead the blaring horns!
This tiny space is but a glimpse of what was here before;
The aspen's gentle moan has fallen top the motor's roar.
What was is soon to be forgot;
   What is to come few can erase;
    O mourn what God cannot replace
In an empty acre lot!

Let It Drop

Father, Father, In the sky!
        I beg of you to make it drop!
My grass is dead, please hear my cry,
        That loaded raincloud needs to drop!
The sky is dark, but still no rain;
The air is filled with sandy grain;
Please ease us from the horrid pain
        Or I will die, Lord
            I will die!
But yet be still my crying tongue:
        The wind blows harder from its lung;
A flash of light, the look of night,
        The thunder borne of clouds has rung!
A touch of cold I now behold,
        It makes its way on down my cheek,
This is no tear that trickles here
        But the wet lifeblood of a creek!
And hark, O ear, it sounds like leaves;
        Lord God is crying on the plain!
My sorrowed conscience no more grieves;
        I cannot see for all the rain!

Father, Father, in the sky!
I beg of you, don't let it stop!
Fill up the creeks, leave nothing dry
And let it not let up or stop!
The air is wet and dust is mud,
The heart of earth welcomes its blood,
But please, O Lord, Don't let it flood
Or I will die, Lord,
I will die!
So please be still, my dancing feet,
And lips now think before you greet.
This is not right, that from this height
My heavy feet can water meet!
I hear a sound from lower ground
And slowly turn, heart pumping blood,
And O so near, I watch in fear
My needed rain turn into flood.
So rushing now it comes my way
And I know devils made this rain!
O save me, Lord, I am its prey!
I can't escape from all the rain!

Father, Father, in the sky!
I beg of you to make it stop!
I'll soon be dead, please hear my cry,
And make this evil madness stop!
The house is gone and all the floor,
My shrinking hill is just a shore,
O please, my Father, nothing more!
Or I will die, Lord,
I will die!
But just be still, my wagging tongue,
The tides without relent are flung.
It looks as though the water flow
Will take this hill to which I've clung.
My lovely land is but the sand
That is the floor beneath the flood.
Where roamed the deer is no more here,
Where I did work and shed my blood!
And now nowhere I have to run,
For gone is all the sprawling plain;
O Father high, here comes your son,
I cannot breathe for all the rain!

Make Me An Image of My Love

O mind, make me an image of my love
While sleep has drawn the curtains on my sight;
Release the hand bound by this battered glove
That I might hold her once again tonight.
For she has fled, as darkness during day,
Ascended up forbidden flights of stairs,
But time, that thief, this vision cannot slay
That, ageless, spiteless, never ceases cares.
If only dreams were life! Those spectral eyes
Have shipwrecked me and washed me to her coast,
And I, at last, again will hear the sighs
Of love; if not the woman, then the ghost!
Lie, Mind, restore me to our love's lost youth,
And let me not awake to know the truth!

Misty Rain

So lonely, sad, and freezing cold
While riding on a strange terrain,
A pleasant mem'ry I behold
Of beauty like I can't explain,
        Where cattle graze
        On summer days
And misty rain falls on the plain.

Another place, another time,
When I was not I hired hand,
But so much more, back in my prime
When there was less to understand,
        But now I'm here
        With cow and steer
And riding on another's land.

I dream of rolling hills tonight;
A wish I know is wished in vain,
Where nightime stars are more than bright
And men live by the sun and rain.
        And yet I grieve,
        I want to leave;
O take me there to ride again.

But though I know this place exists,
Slim is the chance I'll ever go;
The reins forever cuff my wrists
And time remains my greatest foe.

So must I stay
So far away
And try these dreams to overthrow?

But something in the starry sky
Leaves me a thought to entertain,
And then I know before I die
I'll ride that sprawling range again
Where cattle graze
On summer days
And misty rain falls on the plain.

MOVE AWAY

Move away into the country—that's the place to be
For there the forests roll away into eternity.
So act right now, to claim your open space, and fast
For these five-acre tracts aren't likely long to last.
Leave city strife and hurried life to now be free
And move away to see all that there is to see!

Days come and go and yet these pamphlets never die
And each new house but clutters space and clutters open sky.
Therefore we hope amid our herds that it will pass
But still more come, persistent as the grass.

No doubt the tide will slow,
And no doubt the cancerous tumor cease to grow,
But at what cost, for on one day they'll waken and behold
The horrid face of change and feel their hearts grow cold,
Then seek another haven where their hearts feel freed
And again the call of move out to the country heed.

On Looking At A Picture of the Earth

I'm down there somewhere. Somewhere past the clouds
I stand, not knowing future eyes of mine
Are watching over me among the crowds
Of people, on this ball of God's design.

Here night and day are seen at once; men sleep
In Oregon, men wake in Germany,
Magellan's Strait feels summer heat, the deep
Snow drowns Montana, all in harmony.

Our greatest castles, buildings, tracts of land,
Are nothing from up here; just moss on a
Cathedral wall. No structure made by hand
Decries the painted pearl; no worth to weigh.

But even though the stage is beautiful,
The play is much more boring from this seat.
To live the action is more great; to rule,
To live, to act this play without repeat.

It will outlive us all, and when we come
To heaven's walls, we'll feel for it no more.
But something makes me wonder; visions from
A dream: is this the view from heaven's door?

Padre Island

There is a place among the brush I know
Down where the prairies roll to meet the sea,
Where hills recede and rivers gently flow
Past land and deep into infinity,
And there a soul will brood on times gone by,
And times to come, and times that never came
Beneath the rolling rush of leaves that cry
"Here none are great; here are no thrones for fame."

It has been long, yes, ages since the time
That I last heard the sounding wave despair;
I dwell within a harsh and altered clime
And watch the loss and thinning of my hair.
Therefore at times I long once more to be
Upon that plain to know tranquillity;
To wonder there, as waves rush back to me:
What else is love, What else is ecstasy?

SALT LAKE CITY

If in Salt Lake, one cannot help but feel
An awe; a vanity of human might
Among those streets, those palaces of steel
Like gems that shine as beacons in the night,
For now their inaccessibility
Is overthrown as these do void defy,
And in this pith, the temple too does free
Its spires in exhaltation to the sky.

But should one look from those, and higher still,
And then behold the solemn majesty
That is the mountains, ageless in the sky they fill,
One might then gain, if one should glance and see
Those sticks, no more than stakes in salty sod,
A reckoning of what man is to God.

The Brand

Hold not against me what I feel,
Dear Mother, for this ageless plain;
My heart could no more this repeal
Than leaves could of the dew complain.

For we belong not to ourselves
But to some other, greater plan
As grass, from dust, from dew, but delves
Into the cattle of the man.

A man, who brands them at a whim;
A mark meant for eternity,
And thus, so have I branded them,
So has this prairie branded me.

The Chapel

When I was young, when I was free,
In younger days of history,
This man was strong, his heart was gold,
But of the Lord he'd not been told.
And so I rode, and rode, and rode,
Working on the unbeaten road,
For unknown brands in unknown lands,
From coastal plains to desert sands.

With empty hearts I wasted love
And never saw the hidden dove,
Went roaming through the wilderness
In apathy and carelessness
Until my boots stepped on the sand
That robed the miles of hilly land,
And with the shaking of a hand,
The maverick wore an unseen brand.

I rode that day like days before
Upon the grassy prairie floor,
Then in the cedars by the stream
There was a calf whose eyes did gleam,
Having foot rot or some disease
Ever stopping to cough or sneeze.
To help him feel well was my hope;
My hand went down and clutched my rope.

Then heading for the cedar trees,
Through live oak trees and autumn breeze,
I chased after the running cow
As fast as horseflesh would allow,
And coming close I threw my rope
And proudly saw the nylon grope,
But slipped my dallies from my hand,
And went the calf on through the land.

Then through the hills and live oak trees
With nylon rope drug at his knees,
My little calf ran down the creek
With no more sign of being weak,
And watching him run through the rock
While blood was smearing at his hock,
I knew what this came to amount,
To follow him I must dismount.

So afoot I traveled quickly,
Looking for this calf so sickly,
Climbing up in elevation,
Increasing in desolation,
And though the rocks around increased,
I would not have this cow deceased,
When I could help and rescue him
Before the sunlight has gone dim.

And, O so close, my need was now,
My feet were almost to the cow,
But running through a pair of trees,
He vanished like the autumn breeze.

I then sat down upon the ground
And listened to the earth around,
And getting back off of my knees,
I stepped on through the double trees.

Then all was quiet and serene
And still, in cold, the leaves were green;
No birds sang here, none dare disturb
The peaceful chapel none perturb.
The chapel where the creek began,
The chapel where my cow had ran,
And balanced on the rocky sod,
I shed a tear,
and felt my God.

The way the sun shone on the grass
Was like the beauty of stained glass;
The limestone walls a vaulted roof,
Of His existence that was proof,
And all around the windy choir,
Away from light and road and wire,
Sang their hymn of the God above
And whispered of undying love.

I felt then of another tear
And asked my Father, "Are you here?"
And from the silence all the wind
Made all the live oaks start to bend.
I laughed and cried and danced around,
My place in life I knew I'd found;

The pillared trees, the starting stream
Were like the landscape of a dream.

I stayed there for another hour
And listened to the windy choir,
But soon the sunset in the sky
Forced me to leave, for night was nigh.
I carried my calf out of there,
Still feeling of that holy air,
And at the trees I made a turn,
And whispered back,
"I will return."

II

Now, here I am, a weak old man
Whose tan complexion has gone wan,
With shuffling step, I walk the land;
I hold a cane and not a brand.
But still it haunts me in my dreams,
That place, the mother of all streams,
Where all is quiet and serene
And all the grass is always green.

Today I felt the call again
To flee this world of lust and sin
And take myself out to the hills
Where stand the cattle and windmills,
And to that place I chose to drive
Where everything feels so alive;

I left my truck beside the road
And went to where that lost creek flowed.

My knees were hurting, needed rest,
But still to me this was a test
If I could be there one more time
Before I fell to Father Time.
So, once again through rocky hills,
I was reliving youthful thrills;
Stumbling, chasing, like a sleuth
The fleeing calf that is my youth.

Stopping just to catch my breath
To keep away my coming death,
I stumbled upward with my cane
On rocks well moistened by the rain,
And slipping once, I feared the fall
From height so high my skin would crawl,
But clutching trees, I made my way
Back to the warm light of the day.

And there they stood: the double trees;
Once again I fell to my knees
And praised my Father high above,
For I knew now of all His love.
I walked again to those old trees
That kept away the chilling breeze,
And pulling back the limbs so smooth,
A dying man revived his youth.

This place of God had never changed
And still the hills forever ranged
And still the mighty limestone walls
Looked like massive cathedral halls.
Slipping, slipping, on all the rocks
Like the calf with the bloody hocks,
And weak and old, with splintered rod,
I cried again,
and felt my God.

Then all the leaves became alive,
And this alone was worth the drive;
The pillared trees swayed to the wind,
My broken heart began to mend.
And still today the water flows
And still today the live oak grows
And now today I am complete;
Today my Father I will meet.

I then sit down with dying pain
And put beside me my old cane
To feel the power of His love
While it's descending from above.
I lay my head against the dirt
And watch the leaves blow on my shirt.
A natural man in nature's arm
Forever safe, forever warm.

I know not if they'll find me here
But if they don't I will not fear;
Today I go to see the throne,
A loner who will die alone.
I look again into the trees
And feel the soothing, loving breeze,
Then all I hear, like birds on fly,
Are flapping wings,
And then I die.

The Cowboy Considers Immortality

Why should we cherish immortality,
When from conception, we embark a quest,
And struggle through the thorns from East to West,
To catch that calf that none for long can see;
To cast away the sword and follow rest?

No, for if suddenly God deemed us power
To, like the sea, throughout the ages sweep,
Not like a desert stream to dry and creep,
Regard the century an idle hour,
A thousand years we would then spend in sleep.

The Cowboy Speaks of His Love

Much are the scenes that have my eyes allured:
The peaks by Winter's icy hands caressed,
The languid plain, the vales along the quest
Of shifting birds by summer's kisses lured.
Yet never was I lost, my goal obscured,
Nor were my wits in chaos dispossessed,
But for the constant path made manifest
By bright Polaris in the North secured.
Such is this little world, and such our love,
That never we shall breathe again forlorn,
For love is but the beacon bright whereof
The cruelest heart shall fail to shun its bourne.
So shall it always be, lest stars distill;
So come, and let love lead us where it will.

The Cowboy To His City Love

My love, how terrible that we should meet
At this dim hour, with only power to stare
Across the fence between the land and street.
The sun has fallen; wind breathes through our hair,
And in the distance, lights begin to flare
Within the households of your world. You say
Your arms are warmer than the night, You care
More than the cattle; Come with me, you say?
My horse stands waiting–Do I go or stay?

Oh, that I had been born to different soles,
We two could kiss, and to each other clutch
Forever, but we must act out our roles.
How God must laugh that we would love so much,
That you would choose my hand of coarser touch,
Though richer men for you have bent their knee!
Why me? My life is cursed to bear a crutch,
And like the whale imprisoned by the sea,
The bonds that snare us will not let us free.

But yet I love you! Bright Orion's flare
Holds nothing to your eyes; my seas of grass
Are worthless to the acre of your hair;
The rain more savage than your tears. I pass
These thoughts away; the sun can't have his lass,
The moon, though every day he makes a try
To hold her, his vast warmth cannot surpass
Her cold, and he is swallowed by her sky!
Observe! This is the way in which dreams die!

Be gone, and leave me to my grazing herd!
Go to your ashes, leave me to my dust!
It is a shame our ears had ever heard
The whispers of each other's voice; we must
Obey the callings of our deeper lust.
Release me, woman! Run and hide from me,
But know that I will hear in every gust
Your name, though by tomorrow you shall be
Still loved, still graced, but yet still lost to me.

The Horse Without A Rider

My heart is free of all that shone in open ways
    of pride and glee;
I only see the sweating horse whose seat
    lies barren before me,
For somewhere in the mountain shades
    the soulfire of another fades
        And blood will merge with callous sand
        And dust returns unto the land.
O saddle light, and cold and barren,
Reins that dangle so forgotten,
Where is your leather armored baron?
Is his skin still soft or rotten?
I do not know, for loose the seeds
    of life and death are thrown,
And every journey that we take
    is with great peril strewn.
Hence wearied horse, please take me there,
    and let me for my partner weep
        And all will pass in nightly sleep,
        When we bury him alone and deep.

So let the mountains magnify until
we reach our journey's end
For that unknown nearby or where
the sky and skyline blend.
But cattle cannot ever speak
and thus again my heart is weak
Because I cannot find the man
From whose parting you have ran.
O faithful horse, so low on breath,
How black the skies from buzzards grow
From fuming smells of newborn death
And to their feathers I will go.
But how I fear in saddest thoughts
that he is lying past the fence;
Before it lies an endless sea
of sharp mesquite and cactus dense.
If so, our dream has finished,
and the things for which we yearn
And all our fears in ashes burn
Beneath a sun unable to return.

The Oaks of Hemphill Prairie

You solemn oaks, observers of an age,
Deep rooted guardians of sweet nature's being,
In wooden countenance, whose arms will rage
And flail to grasp the autumn dead leaves fleeing;
Castles, as high within your leafy towers
The scissortail and mockingbird converse,
And glare at man, with all his savage powers
That would annihilate what he should nurse.

And did the cowboy rest here on his trails
As I do here? And at his death, your wood,
Did it his dust embrace and bear his nails,
Decay and fall with him, as like things should?
Then this is but a scene seen much before,
Where, on the ground with your sent blessings dressed,
A herdsman from his weary world will pour
Into the shadowed realm of easeful rest.

Rest, for like rootless seeds, so have I wandered,
As you my steadfast oaks, in restless youth;
Compelled by whims beyond control, I pondered:
Why, why must toil unwanted be my truth?
To root, to spread, and to the sky aspire,
Unhampered by the winds harsh in their sway;
In inner peace, not discontent, to tire,
As you, what man these wishes turns away?

For look, from up the veils of tangled leaves,
A leaf is blown, unnoticed, from the limb,
And falls to earth, wilts, while the wood unweaves,
And leaves its passing to the memory dim.
In this way do the hours seem to fly:
So tranquil, that the first dead pass unmourned,
Until, too late, what once in love did sigh
Can but rattle in splendor unadorned.

So teach, impeccable, how one can stand
Contented constant, never once to see
Or wish the mystery of a foreign land!
Teach us, to conquer the obscurity
Within this tenebrous world beneath the leaves
Where sun is felt but seldom awes the eye;
Enlighten us, who shift as shadowed thieves,
To no more dwell as strangers to the sky.

For I have cherished, when amidst the air
Of dismal city streets, with men who bawl
As fresh-weaned calves these woods, and unaware
Passed by the fear, the beggar in her shawl;
The wolves that horde and stalk those frozen timbers;
Cherished, as do the cattle prize the grass
This vision, as the heart there fond remembers
A grace no lover's whisper could surpass.

For then your memory awakened me
As when sweet spring has kissed the barren bough,
Or when one old has read in levity
A lover's letter written long ago.

Yet parting warned mortality, for then
Each parting stride an evanescence seemed;
Each glance away November's poison;
The dawn's approach when one has softly dreamed.

The wind with careless hands impels once more,
The seed sinks from the leaf unto the lake,
Disturbs the mirrored calm, and to the shore,
The silver rings increaseth, swell, and shake,
Then fade away, as stars before the sun,
That one must ask if they were there at all.
Thus are we, trees, a shimmer scarce begun
Before our deeds seem shadowed by a pall.

And wood we are, both bound by solid bands
Of endless years grown heavy on our souls,
Which have concealed, as cities under sands,
The wounds the architect unkindly doles;
Wood, such as to be whittled by the blade,
and severed, forced our pleasures to desist;
Cast from quintessence, fashioned to be made
A totem or a doorstop to exist.

But this we know-dead trees no shelter yield,
But in the darkness warm the frozen heart,
Encase our cares, give cause to hands that build
Eternal monuments of highest art,
And pages make, that poets dead may sing,
And long endure, though natures may arraign,
Or like the staff of Moses, radiance bring
Into the darkness of the Sinai plain.

Still stands your shape against the driving gale;
Still firm your roots adhere to brittle earth,
Yet even still, as with a golden sail,
The sun descends unto his western berth,

And I, for fear of fever, chill, or death
Must mournfully unto my home retreat,
While these same limbs which waver with a breath,
Endure the force that would my shell defeat.

How sad it is that cow or stolid deer
And every beast unworthier than I,
In peaceable repose, come cloud or clear,
May long partake in this incessant sigh!
How sad, how grievous, how unkind to know
That Nature in her laws stands obstinate,
And in this manner, are we flush with woe,
And baser creatures prove more fortunate.

Away I ride, and these fair scenes regress
Like precious shells beneath the tide immersed;
Too soon my heart, which cried to convalesce,
Departs and shifts among the world dispersed!
Aye, far from these I ride, but yet abide,
As trails forgotten, clothed in lush array,
When hooves, the cowboy's cries, the branded hide,
Have all, like trail dust, passed long since away.

The Shadow Man

There came a horse that bore an empty saddle;
    No rider in its seat;
The leather groaned and coughed stirrup's rattle
    To the horse's beat.
Pulled it was behind a somber man;
    His horse was midnight dark
Beneath the brim his face was tan;
    His features cold and stark.
A charcoal frock coat fluttered on his back;
    A purpose to his gait;
The horses laden each with well worn tack
    And still they were first rate.
Yet still the townsfolk people paid him little mind;
    The fear within me ran
And I shivered at when my mind did find:
    Not one eye could see this man
Save me, a solitary cowboy with a mount;
    Still young and not yet wise
But I could see this man, his horses count
    With my very eyes.
He passed me as I watched him ride
    And both our eyes did meet,
But there was not a place to run or hide
    Upon this dusty street.
But yet it was not me he came for;
    No qualm he had for me
Yet I could only stare and nothing more
    At this man in front of me.
He rode on down the windswept road

At a steady pace
Looking at every building as he rode
For the proper place.
Then at the home of Sam his feet did land;
An old man's home, in truth;
They say old Sam was a top hand
Back in his days ofyouth.
Stove up he was; no longer could he ride
Which grieved his heart so much;
With outlaw horses he had used to ride
And broncos of the such.
Therefore I wondered of what business this man had
With this man grown old;
And if he needed something Ol' Sam had
To walk in so bold.
He tied the reins on to the hitching post
And went inside the door;
My God, he walked with grace like an ancient ghost
Then I could see his form no more.
Within a moments span he walked back out;
I tell you this is true–
Beside him had another man walked out . . .
A man I never knew.
His hair was dark, his face was tanned;
A smile upon his face
His riding boots and spurs stirred up the sand;
On horseback was his place.
The bay he mounted and eased upon the saddle;
This horse unfrightened with his care;
Why, this was a man at home among wild cattle
Out in the windy air.

As they passed by he looked at me;
His eyes were turquoise blue;
He smiled and it occurred to me
That this man I knew.
He then let out a youthful chuckle;
I knew him from his eyes

And how he wore his silver buckle
    Like a huntsman's cherished prize.
The somber man he dared to race;
    A smile replaced his frown;
With youthful fire upon his sun-tanned face
    They sped on out of town.
I pondered then where I had seen this man;
    Was he Sam's son, perhaps?
I thought as I had rode out to my land
    And buckled up my chaps.
Yet I had noticed that the duo's trail had vanished
    About a half a mile from town
Like from reality they had been banished;
    What trail had they gone down?
The question then had plagued me for a week;
    Where had I seen him before?
Had I ever seen him resting by a creek
    Or at the general store?
The week passed by, and I returned to town
    Where I was at before;
Sam's home was empty, closed, shut down
    With boards across the door.
In shock, in fright, I grabbed a friend who hurried by
    And pointed to Sam's home,
And in his tender ear I rung this startled cry:
    "To where did old Sam roam?!"
He sighed, then through his mouth he spread the word:
    "You mean that you don't know?"
"Why, son," said he, " I thought you heard . . .
    He died a week ago . . ."

The Trail's Philosophy

If nothing else, my life has taught me this:
There is no end to learning, but a yearning
That lingers like the Guadalupe churning
Forever onward to some far abyss.
And like that river, which could with a tear
Embark upon endeavors so severe
That ancient oaks unanchor from the earth,
So is our mind, which, to increase its girth,
Drains tributaries numberless and grown,
Unaided, reckless, flows to parts unknown.

I was then once that trickle ere the flood
And found myself amid the hooves that marred
A trail, a river in its own regard,
For ardent was the passion of my blood.
And destitute my soul was then, and free
Before me was this trail; a mystery,
But I knew naught of perils imminent.
Therefore by night I rode, for incontent
Was I, to like the cattle, blindly trail,
And asked my boss to of the miles foretell.

How can I speak of this, he said, when drives,
Like days, like lives, run with inconstancy?
For never sun with such a frequency
Did linger that, whereon his heat arrives,
One knew the measure of his task.
No, we are cursed with plague, for from the flask

Of God could come stampedes, or hail, or death,
Or drives that smoothly run as autumn's breath.
But know, the town will come, when sun shall nest,
For which one lives to dream, to sing, to rest.

Thereat he rode, but deep within the blaze
That bathed the camp at night I tore his dream,
Until at last, the lights of Dodge did seem
The flame one sees when death is near; the days
Before, their peril, but a hazy blur.
It is because of this that I prefer
To think of death not as the night, but yet
That town, and though the soul may cry regret,
Far near the sky is cause for which to sing,
A hope, a dream; a new awakening.

THE TREE

In youth I saw a tree among a score;
Beheld it by a bolt from heaven struck,
And through its limbs a horrid glory snuck,
Engulfed the night, but touched the flame no more.

I watched in fear, in awe, the blazes claim
The fruit, and all else that the boughs bestow,
Though in a hour extinguished was its flame
And if it lived or died I do not know.

This I perceived as greatness, although brief,
Inspired by chance, with winds to judge its fate,
For that one tree had gained in every leaf
The power to destroy and create,
And would, if dead, be passed in high regard,
And had it lived, remain forever scarred.

To A Hawk

Three times this day, O hawk, have I beheld your wings
While on my futile, wild, and ceaseless wanderings,
Compelled to fancy and to dream a dream that we,
Though born apart, bore hearts that beat in harmony
And in the spaces that know naught of builder's hand,
Unhurt by thoughts of what our time and age has planned,
We go where chance, not fate, will lead with wings unfurled
And fly beyond the wickedness of this our world.

But one must always wake from foolish dreams, and I,
Though grieved, must too descend and bid farewell to sky
And walk irresolute, uncertain if I meet
Again these hills, these snow-capped peaks, when but a beat
Of feathered wings for you these woes of mine defeat.
Were that I were as you, not to this vessel bound,
Held captive by my thoughts, my fears secured around
A soul by conscience bound and friend to misery;
I might know peace to know the wild's serenity;
To cry, and hear my echoes calling from afar
And no more brood upon what love and freedom are.

Tomorrow

There is a crest of land which rises to the east
Which has a face no man that I have known has seen of pieced
Together fragments of its mystery. For some the passion
burned
And they have climbed its shoulder and scuttled to the other
side, but they have not returned.
Tomorrow I will go and see what their forgotten eyes have seen,
To dwell and think upon the folding waves of green
Hued mountains that have felt their boots, and rippling
tongues that they must speak.
I think of these things I will know when I shall conquer
yonder peak.

There are some that tell me of the sea; the words breathe
strange new blood into my veins;
They say it is an inundation vast and endless as the plains;
A place where molten gold floats on the water
as the sky-fire falls;
That breeds such mythic things as waterspouts and squalls.
Tomorrow, I shall see where the great fireball is spewed up
from the earth
And watch the shiny droplets reflect upon the shades of that
which gave them birth.

I know the old men have never climbed the wall to see
    what world awaits;
They have spoken only words passed down with liquor
    by their mates.
Tomorrow then, how great my grief shall be, if, at the apex
    of my quest
I should look to find the wastelands just continue
    past the crest.

But even then I shall trudge on, and die to please my eyes
And cross each crest and trough till blue
    are both the earth and skies.
I think I hear the sea birds now; I cannot tell
    if they are laughing or crying;
Soon the sky will spit the flame again and I'll not need
    these embers that are dying.
Tomorrow I will stand and I will sing,
    and all the earth and heaven will know my name,
And all will know I've found the prize
    that is the reason that I came.
Tomorrow I will rise and I will find my fugitive.
Tomorrow I will leave my footprints in the sand
    and stare across the sea.
Tomorrow I will live.

We Are The Men

We are the men beyond the fence
Who are but shadows to the world,
We ride where men are not as dense
And ride with rawhide ropes uncurled,
Men known throughout in worldly lore
Riding in a beaten saddle,
Working with our herds of cattle,
Riding just to brave the battle,
Until the day when we can ride no more.

We are the men who wear the spur,
Who wear the bullhide on our leg,
And read the brands marked on the fur,
And to the sky for rain we beg.
From leaves we hear the whispered roar
When winter brings the northern wind,
A sound we hope will never end,
And from the cold our hats we bend
Until the day when we can ride no more.

But all decays like autumn leaves
And cedar fenceposts by the road,
The minutes are like stealthy thieves
And we forget how proud we rode.
We mourn, and yet forevermore
Beyond the fence they watch us ride,
And marvel at the branded hide
But from their ways we try to hide
Until the day when we can ride no more.

Behind the fence with weary eyes
    As helpless twigs upon a dream
We watch the road and cluttered skies
    Behind the brick, behind the steam.
Though that day comes which we deplore,
    We cannot stop or slow our sun,
    And through the days we seem to run
    Against our will and fear when done
The day that we shall ride no more.

We Yearned to Live

The old time rancher yearned to live my life.
It was his dream, it was his life-long quest
To shoot no more and put away his knife
And live to see a safer, tamer West.
His was the West before the fence and road,
His boots knew more of stirrup skin than grass,
He lived when undammed rivers freely flowed,
Forever riding till these things would pass.
Hot days, dark nights, he knew of all of these
And for a while he thought the herding way
Unfit to live, there could be much more ease
With cities close and not so far away.
In hope, he lay beneath the stars each night
And wished to them for better days to come,
And while the cattle grazed, the evening light
Lit all the range, and in his dreams he swum.
Someday, he knew, the red man would not haunt
Behind the shadows of the trees in rage.
His brand would live, he would be free of want,
He would be free to smell the sweetened sage.
But yet he died along the northward trail,
While on the plains the untrod moon did gleam.
Beneath the trampling hooves he raised, he fell,
And never knew the nightmare of his dream.

I yearn to live the old time rancher's life.
It is my dream, it is my life-long quest.
I think of them when I unfold my knife
To cut one of the cattle of the West.
Mine is the West that saw his dream fulfilled,
I ride behind the barbed wire fence they built
And now around me all their homes they build
On former range, but yet they have no guilt.
The trail is paved with concrete for the cars
With fences stretching by its side. At night
The sky is bright with lights that dim the stars
And they wish all the horsemen from their sight.
A wind picks up and whispered echoes come
In from the hills, and then I hear a part
Of voices dead and things that yip and drum.
I hear his call, and know his broken heart.
If only we could switch our saddles, we
Would have our dream, and we would make it last,
For different times have different dreams, you see;
He lived for future, I live for the past.
We ride on separate sides of barbed wire fence,
We cannot reach each other's trails. We don
Our gear, and though I often feel a sense
Of him, we cannot meet, and we ride on.

What The Cow Said

In truth, I live long after I am dead
And on the skin of different legs I've tread
The land where hooves could not have taken me
And I have helped a nation reach their sea.
A thousand kings have felt me on their backs
And I have seen all wars on swords and packs,
And after I had walked the northward course,
The next year I returned, but on a horse.
I've battled cold, and babes æround me have curled,
And I have whipped the traitors of the world.

How great my life has been, short though it be,
For I, in stretched steel bondage, have been free
To graze on grasses sweetened by the dew
Without the savage teeth of wolves in view.
My worth has not been wasted; in time's span
Of lasting, I am worth much more than man.
To live in paradise, I lost the wild,
And died to feed the world and starving child,
And gave the strength to walk to those who crawl,
And I can say that it was worth it all.

I Leave You Now

I leave you now, to go my separate way
But let my natural name escape you not,
For all this time that we have shared this day
Should not so soon be wasted and forgot.
Tonight the wind will come erase my prints
That lie in dust indented by my heels,
When sunlight fades to change to twilight tints
And all have drove away on rubber wheels.
Yes, all shall blow away in time like dust
And every sign that I was even here;
All vanishes before the Northern gust
Except these words that rode into your ear;
These tales, these sagas of our dying life,
From longhorn trails to herdsmen of today;
For they have cut your soul with Goodnight's knife
And brought you to another time and day.
But if you leave this place with empty hearts,
Their message dies out like the Chisholm trail
And then another part of us departs
Then who is left to tell you of our tale?
Farewell, I leave, and peace be with you all:
The sun is setting off towards the West.
Tomorrow I will ride where ranges sprawl
To live a life with which I am obsessed.
But know these words, and spread them through the world
Of cows, of spurs; the land where storms have whirled,
And spread these words as leaves fly from a tree;
Tell these, so that we might remembered be.

ABOUT THE AUTHOR

JEREMIAH LEIF PICKETT JOHNSON, a fifth generation working cowboy, was born in 1979 in the Big Thicket of East Texas. Born to a heritage including ranchers, Native Americans, Texas Rangers and outlaws he writes with the concerns of his generation in a west where ranching fades with each new year.

By the time he entered eighth grade what was later to become his hold on poetry was already taking shape. Already passionate in acting since the fourth grade, Johnson performed in a myriad of plays and productions ranging from Galveston's Dickens on the Strand to the Texas Renaissance Festival. His discovery of poetry was mingled with this passion and gave birth to his style of writing which is still maturing today.

In 1993 Johnson's family merged their emu operation and South Texas ranching operation to a Central Texas cattle ranch outside of Bastrop. After holding his first paying job as a working cowboy with the Lentz Cattle Company, Johnson grew ever closer to the ranching life and began to write of the sadness within his heart. Within four months his work appeared in *American Cowboy* Magazine, beginning a new era in his life in cowboy poetry.

In 1997 Johnson was nominated for the AWA's Rising Star award and has since received many national and international awards for his literary achievements. He has been featured with such notables as Red Steagall and Don Edwards. He continues to travel across North America with his work and now resides on his family's ranch on the prairies north of Goliad, Texas.

Website: http://www.angelfire.com/tx/cowboypoet/

ABOUT THE ARTISTS

LARRY BUTE, who followed his destiny to the windswept valleys of Nevada, has ridden for several ranches in Wyoming, Montana, and Nevada researching the northern buckaroo. His distinct style has appeared in many magazines and murals and he has illustrated publications for such western names as Waddie Mitchell and the Tonto Rim Trading Co. Praised for his sharp eyes and his ability to bring what he has seen to life, he says of his beloved cowboy life: "It's the only kind of life I want to live."

As a personal note, Larry's depiction of the four distinct types of working cowmen in America indirectly led to my involvement in cowboy poetry when it inspired me to write my first published work. I am forever grateful to him for agreeing to this task.

MARK KOHLER, a painter based in Central Texas, has travelled from Argentina to Montana studying and painting the cowboy at work and at rest. A former student of Peña, his work with watercolor has been praised by many and has appeared as the illustrations for the 1998 Santa Clarita Cowboy Poetry Gathering and others. His attention to detail, particularly to the facial characteristics, is unique and seldom seen in Western Art.